FRANCIS FRITH'S

TENBY AND SAUNDERSFOOT

PHOTOGRAPHIC MEMORIES

MARION DAVIES BA, PGCE, MITG was a model maker and teacher before becoming a self-employed Wales Blue Badge Guide, chiefly engaged in a variety of themed guided walks around the historic town of Tenby; she also offers guided tours further afield. She has contributed to a variety of radio and television programmes, and in 2003 she wrote *A Guide to Tenby and Saundersfoot* which was edited by Mark Lewis.

MARK LEWIS BA is a published poet, writer and playwright; he achieved considerable local acclaim for his play based on the life of the artist Gwen John. A regular contributor to magazines and the author of various literary articles, he is the Assistant Curator at Tenby Museum and Art Gallery, where he has worked for 10 years.

FRANCIS FRITH'S
PHOTOGRAPHIC MEMORIES

TENBY AND SAUNDERSFOOT

PHOTOGRAPHIC MEMORIES

MARION DAVIES
AND MARK LEWIS

First published in the United Kingdom in 2004 by
The Francis Frith Collection

Limited Hardback Subscribers Edition Published in 2004
ISBN 1-85937-813-7

Paperback Edition 2004
ISBN 1-85937-662-2

Text and Design copyright © The Francis Frith Collection
Photographs copyright © The Francis Frith Collection

The Frith photographs and the Frith logo are reproduced under licence from Heritage Photographic Resources Ltd, the owners of the Frith archive and trademarks

All rights reserved. No photograph in this publication may be sold to a third party other than in the original form of this publication, or framed for sale to a third party. No parts of this publication may be reproduced, stored in a retrieval system, or transmitted, in any form, or by any means, electronic, mechanical, photocopying, recording or otherwise, without the prior permission of the publishers and copyright holder.

British Library Cataloguing in Publication Data

Francis Frith's Tenby and Saundersfoot - Photographic Memories
Marion Davies and Mark Lewis

The Francis Frith Collection
Frith's Barn, Teffont,
Salisbury, Wiltshire SP3 5QP
Tel: +44 (0) 1722 716 376
Email: info@francisfrith.co.uk
www.francisfrith.com

Printed and bound in Great Britain

Front Cover: **TENBY**, *South Sands 1890* 28050t
Frontispiece: **TENBY**, *High Street 1950* T23058

The colour-tinting is for illustrative purposes only, and is not intended to be historically accurate

AS WITH ANY HISTORICAL DATABASE THE FRITH ARCHIVE IS CONSTANTLY BEING CORRECTED AND IMPROVED AND THE PUBLISHERS WOULD WELCOME INFORMATION ON OMISSIONS OR INACCURACIES

CONTENTS

FRANCIS FRITH: VICTORIAN PIONEER	7
TENBY AND SAUNDERSFOOT - AN INTRODUCTION	10
TENBY: THE NORTH BAY	16
TENBY: CASTLE HILL, CASTLE BEACH, ST CATHERINE'S ISLAND AND THE ESPLANADE	20
TENBY: INSIDE AND OUTSIDE THE WALLS	32
TENBY: THE HARBOUR	40
CALDEY	46
SAUNDERSFOOT	50
AMROTH AND WISEMAN'S BRIDGE	64
CLIFFS, CAVES AND COVES	68
THE CASTLES OF CAREW AND MANORBIER	74
THE BURROWS, GUMFRESTON AND PENALLY	82
INDEX	89
NAMES OF SUBSCRIBERS	90
Free Mounted Print Voucher	93

DEDICATION

With many thanks for all their help to Charles, Jimmy and David Crockford of Tenby Harbour and also Josh and Peter Richards, Roscoe Howells, Tenby Town Council and Tenby Museum and Art Gallery and all the people of Tenby and Saundersfoot who have helped in so many ways over the years.

And especially to Theo.

FRANCIS FRITH
VICTORIAN PIONEER

FRANCIS FRITH, founder of the world-famous photographic archive, was a complex and multi-talented man. A devout Quaker and a highly successful Victorian businessman, he was philosophical by nature and pioneering in outlook.

By 1855 he had already established a wholesale grocery business in Liverpool, and sold it for the astonishing sum of £200,000, which is the equivalent today of over £15,000,000. Now a very rich man, he was able to indulge his passion for travel. As a child he had pored over travel books written by early explorers, and his fancy and imagination had been stirred by family holidays to the sublime mountain regions of Wales and Scotland. 'What lands of spirit-stirring and enriching scenes and places!' he had written. He was to return to these scenes of grandeur in later years to 'recapture the thousands of vivid and tender memories', but with a different purpose. Now in his thirties, and captivated by the new science of photography, Frith set out on a series of pioneering journeys up the Nile and to the Near East that occupied him from 1856 until 1860.

INTRIGUE AND EXPLORATION

These far-flung journeys were packed with intrigue and adventure. In his life story, written when he was sixty-three, Frith tells of being held captive by bandits, and of fighting 'an awful midnight battle to the very point of surrender with a deadly pack of hungry, wild dogs'. Wearing flowing Arab costume, Frith arrived at Akaba by camel sixty years before Lawrence of Arabia, where he encountered 'desert princes and rival sheikhs, blazing with jewel-hilted swords'.

He was the first photographer to venture beyond the sixth cataract of the Nile. Africa was still the mysterious 'Dark Continent', and Stanley and Livingstone's historic meeting was a decade into the future. The conditions for picture taking confound belief. He laboured for hours in his wicker dark-room in the sweltering heat of the desert, while the volatile chemicals fizzed dangerously in their trays. Back in London he exhibited his photographs and was 'rapturously cheered' by members of the Royal Society. His reputation as a photographer was made overnight.

VENTURE OF A LIFE-TIME

Characteristically, Frith quickly spotted the opportunity to create a new business as a specialist publisher of photographs. He lived in an era of immense and sometimes violent change.

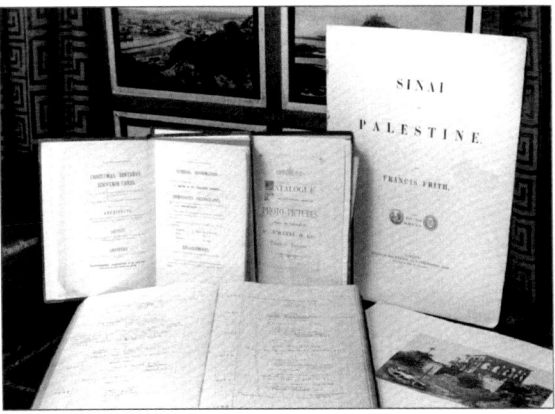

For the poor in the early part of Victoria's reign work was exhausting and the hours long, and people had precious little free time to enjoy themselves. Most had no transport other than a cart or gig at their disposal, and rarely travelled far beyond the boundaries of their own town or village. However, by the 1870s the railways had threaded their way across the country, and Bank Holidays and half-day Saturdays had been made obligatory by Act of Parliament. All of a sudden the working man and his family were able to enjoy days out and see a little more of the world.

With typical business acumen, Francis Frith foresaw that these new tourists would enjoy having souvenirs to commemorate their days out. In 1860 he married Mary Ann Rosling and set out on a new career: his aim was to photograph every city, town and village in Britain. For the next thirty years he travelled the country by train and by pony and trap, producing fine photographs of seaside resorts and beauty spots that were keenly bought by millions of Victorians. These prints were painstakingly pasted into family albums and pored over during the dark nights of winter, rekindling precious memories of summer excursions.

THE RISE OF FRITH & CO

Frith's studio was soon supplying retail shops all over the country. To meet the demand he gathered about him a small team of photographers, and published the work of independent artist-photographers of the calibre of Roger Fenton and Francis Bedford. In order to gain some understanding of the scale of Frith's business one only has to look at the catalogue issued by Frith & Co in 1886: it runs to some 670 pages, listing not only many thousands of views of the British Isles but also many photographs of most European countries, and China, Japan, the USA and Canada - note the sample page shown on page 9 from the hand-written Frith & Co ledgers recording the pictures. By 1890 Frith had created the greatest specialist photographic publishing company in the world, with over 2,000 sales outlets - more than the combined number that Boots and WH Smith have today! The picture on the next page shows the Frith & Co display board at Ingleton in the Yorkshire Dales (left of window). Beautifully constructed with a mahogany frame and gilt inserts, it could display up to a dozen local scenes.

POSTCARD BONANZA

The ever-popular holiday postcard we know today took many years to develop. In 1870 the Post Office issued the first plain cards, with a pre-printed stamp on one face. In 1894 they allowed other publishers' cards to be sent through the mail with an attached adhesive halfpenny stamp. Demand grew rapidly, and in 1895 a new size of postcard was permitted called the court card, but there was little room for illustration. In 1899, a year after Frith's death, a new card measuring 5.5 x 3.5 inches became the standard format, but it was not until 1902 that the divided back came into being, so that the address and message could be on one face and a full-size illustration on the other. Frith & Co were in the vanguard of postcard development: Frith's sons Eustace and Cyril continued their father's monumental task, expanding the number of views offered to the public and recording more and more places in Britain, as the coasts and countryside were opened up to mass travel.

Francis Frith had died in 1898 at his villa in Cannes, his great project still growing. The archive he created continued in business for another seventy years. By 1970 it contained over a third of a million pictures showing 7,000 British towns and villages.

FRANCIS FRITH'S LEGACY

Frith's legacy to us today is of immense significance and value, for the magnificent archive of evocative photographs he created provides a unique record of change in the cities, towns and villages throughout Britain over a century and more. Frith and his fellow studio photographers revisited locations many times down the years to update their views, compiling for us an enthralling and colourful pageant of British life and character.

We are fortunate that Frith was dedicated to recording the minutiae of everyday life. For it is this sheer wealth of visual data, the painstaking chronicle of changes in dress, transport, street layouts, buildings, housing, engineering and landscape that captivates us so much today. His remarkable images offer us a powerful link with the past and with the lives of our ancestors.

THE VALUE OF THE ARCHIVE TODAY

Computers have now made it possible for Frith's many thousands of images to be accessed almost instantly. Frith's images are increasingly used as visual resources, by social historians, by researchers into genealogy and ancestry, by architects and town planners, and by teachers involved in local history projects.

In addition, the archive offers every one of us an opportunity to examine the places where we and our families have lived and worked down the years. Highly successful in Frith's own era, the archive is now, a century and more on, entering a new phase of popularity. Historians consider the Francis Frith Collection to be of prime national importance. It is the only archive of its kind remaining in private ownership. Francis Frith's archive is now housed in an historic timber barn in the beautiful village of Teffont in Wiltshire. Its founder would not recognize the archive office as it is today. In place of the many thousands of dusty boxes containing glass plate negatives and an all-pervading odour of photographic chemicals, there are now ranks of computer screens. He would be amazed to watch his images travelling round the world at unimaginable speeds through internet lines.

The archive's future is both bright and exciting. Francis Frith, with his unshakeable belief in making photographs available to the greatest number of people, would undoubtedly approve of what is being done today with his lifetime's work. His photographs depicting our shared past are now bringing pleasure and enlightenment to millions around the world a century and more after his death.

TENBY AND SAUNDERSFOOT
AN INTRODUCTION

TODAY, both Saundersfoot and Tenby are chiefly engaged in the tourist industry. However, despite being only two miles distant, the origins of the resorts are very different.

Tenby, located on the south west coast of Pembrokeshire, is one of the most beautiful and popular holiday locations in Wales and falls within the Pembrokeshire Coast National Park. The town almost certainly started its life on the Castle Hill; it is thought that this was the location of a Celtic Iron Age promontory fort in about 500 BC, and that this settlement eventually gave rise to the town's name, Dinbych y Pysgod, meaning 'little fort of the fishes'. Gradual Anglicization of this name resulted in its more common English name of Tenby. The early inhabitants probably lived in huts on the headland and farmed the surrounding countryside. They had boats, and fished from the sheltered cove where the harbour is located today.

Life changed dramatically with the coming of the Normans in the late 11th century, which completely altered the cultural balance of the area and gave rise to the naming of south west Pembrokeshire as 'Little England beyond Wales'.

Pembroke was the headquarters of Norman control in the area, but a stone castle was built on Tenby's Castle Hill so as to keep watch on the eastern flank of their demesne lands. Attacks by Welsh princes (of varying success and destruction over the years) resulted in the building of a wall around the town in the 13th century between 12 feet and 15 feet high. There were two stretches of wall running in southerly and westerly directions from cliff to cliff. In about 1328, during Edward III's reign, the pier was built, and so was a large outer tower around the South or Southwest Gate, known today as the Five Arches.

In 1457 the walls were increased to their present height by Jasper Tudor, who was then the Earl of Pembroke and guardian of the future Henry VII. Approximately 50 years later, towers and walls were added to the cliff edges within the town at places that were thought to be vulnerable to attack by sea. The square gun tower at the end of St Florence Parade was also added at this time.

Meanwhile, within the protected environment of the town, things were going exceptionally well for the merchants and traders who had established themselves in Tenby. Indeed, the 14th and 15th centuries were the golden age of Tenby's trading era. Despite attacks by pirates and treacherous seas, Tenby's adventurous trade brought in exotic luxury items, highly desirable at home and in towns further up the Bristol Channel. Goods like wine, oil, vinegar, salt, fruits and pitch came from Spain, France and Portugal; timber, flax, horses and hides came from Ireland; and from Devon came goods for the housewife - pewter, brass, haberdashery and pottery. St Mary's Church is a testament to the great wealth that was generated from this trade; its tithes and endowments led to its becoming the largest medieval parish church in Wales.

During the reign of Elizabeth I, it was thought that so many Spanish captains were familiar with the journey to Tenby that the town may succumb to an attack by the Spanish Armada. Fortunately, the attack never came; but war with Spain marked a gradual decline in the trading success of the town, which had significantly deteriorated only 50 years or so later at the outbreak of Civil War. Tenby was occupied by both the Royalists and the Parliamentarians, and suffered attack and siege. It became a part of the rebellion against Cromwell in the second Civil War. Unlike many other towns, it escaped slighting by Parliamentary forces, but nevertheless it suffered badly when war was immediately followed by the plague which swept through the town in about 1650, reducing the population by at least a third. In the years following the plague, the population declined further. Unoccupied houses decayed and crumbled, and Tenby fell into a ruinous state that was only arrested a hundred years later in the mid 18th century with the coming of the seawater craze.

TENBY, *South Shore c1960* T23102

Invalids suffering from a variety of ailments were recommended by enthusiastic doctors to relocate to the seaside for the beneficial health-giving properties of seawater and the sea air. These were members of the wealthy, leisured classes, who were well used to the freedom of travelling abroad. But as the century drew to a close, foreign travel had become too risky. With the French Revolution and the Napoleonic Wars, attention shifted to locations closer to home. Wales was being discovered. With its mild climate, beautiful beaches, ancient ruins and many excursions, Tenby flourished; its remoteness and therefore exclusivity added to its many charms.

The town had fallen into a sad state of decay, so spirited builders were encouraged to build streets of superior houses and hotels, quality properties to house the many visitors. The early 1800s saw an abundance of elegant Georgian terraces spring up in prominent locations, and all with sea views. In 1810 the entrepreneurial Sir William Paxton of Carmarthenshire opened a bath-house that would serve the many needs of the visitor: it provided hot and cold seawater showers and baths, and a cupping and steam room. There were bathing machines on the beaches, with their attendants who were ready to dip even unwilling invalids, and doctors were recommending the drinking of seawater with milk or with port.

Adjoining the bath-house was the Assembly Rooms, a fashionable meeting place for genteel folk who could attend elegant diversions here

SAUNDERSFOOT, *General View c1965* S64049

such as dances and drawing room operas, or drink coffee in the coffee house. All these many luxuries and treatments came at a price far beyond the means of local people, who found themselves effectively banned from using their own beaches between the hours of 8am and 9pm without a bathing machine.

During these decades of change, Tenby was frequented by some of the most famous people of their age. Writers and artists visited, inspired by the picturesque and beautiful town and the surrounding area: these included Daniel Defoe, J M W Turner, George Eliot, Lewis Carroll, Beatrix Potter, and Gwen John - her notorious bohemian brother Augustus John was born in Tenby. As time went by, access to Tenby became easier by road or sea, and with the coming of the railway, Tenby became firmly fixed as a holiday destination for all.

SAUNDERSFOOT stands in the ancient parish of St Issell. St Issell was an early Celtic saint, reputed to have been the father of St Teilo, who was believed to have been responsible for the foundation of Llandaff Cathedral, Cardiff. Sheltered in a peaceful valley, the parish church stands on the outskirts of the village; a church has existed on this site since the 7th century. Parts of the present church buildings date back to the 13th century, and further additions were made in the 14th century. Considerable restoration work was undertaken in the 19th and early 20th centuries.

The modern seaside town of Saundersfoot is relatively new when compared to some of the ancient and medieval towns and settlements nearby. A survey of 1770 identified only Sandersfoot Farm, which was located near the present seafront car park, and a few small dwellings. This land formed part of the large estates belonging to the prominent land-owning Phillips family of Picton Castle. It was not until the advent of the Industrial Revolution that the town began to expand.

There has been a long history of coal mining in the area. Originally coal was mined in bell-shaped pits, which date back to the 14th century, and later from shafts driven into a slope and worked along seams in all directions. This method proved inefficient, and the pits rapidly became unworkable. Yet mining continued. In 1829 Parliament authorised the Saundersfoot Railway and Harbour Company (first proposed in 1828) to construct a harbour at the west end of the bay - this was finished by 1834 - and a 4-foot gauge tramline which would link some of the collieries. Seven local collieries were using jetties at Saundersfoot to export coal by 1846.

The tramways conveyed coal carts that were initially pulled by horses, sometimes with oxen. Uphill was Bonville's Court Colliery, established in 1842. A series of steel chains connected the carts to a winding house at the top of the incline; the weight of the descending laden carts acted as a fulcrum for the empty ones moving up the hill. Tunnels were constructed through the cliffs, connecting Wiseman's Bridge and Coppet Hall (the name is believed to be derived from 'coal pit haul') by a tramline to Saundersfoot. New rails were put down in the 1870s, permitting a locomotive to travel along the line. This line ran along Railway Street (now the Strand).

The Pembrokeshire coalfield produced high-grade anthracite which was over 90% carbon. It became a valuable commodity during the late

18th and early 19th centuries for the workings of various industries, and was exported to many areas. Queen Victoria also apparently insisted upon its use for the Royal Yacht.

Today, Saundersfoot is surrounded by rolling green hills, and it is hard to imagine it as a hive of industry, with the outlying valleys and sleepy villages bustling with activity, filled with smoke and noise. Yet there was an ironworks at Stepaside, and brickworks near Wiseman's Bridge, which was reputed to have made the finest bricks in the country; the National Trust property of Colby Woodland Garden was a nexus of mine workings, the shafts speared deep into the sides of the valley. All these industries brought their finds to Saundersfoot harbour. Boat building flourished:

Francis Beddoe, who built his last boat in 1872, and H L Read, whose yard continued until 1910, were the two main shipwrights in the village, with their yards in Railway Street.

Those investing in Saundersfoot's industries prospered. Charles Ranken Vickerman, a London solicitor, gained control of Bonville's Court Colliery in 1869. Six years earlier he had obtained the Stepaside Ironworks. In 1860 he had acquired Hean Castle, a mansion which had been built on earlier earthworks, and had reconstructed the house into a lavish Victorian residence built in red sandstone.

However, the increased activity in the coalfields in the valleys of south east Wales, combined with the difficulties of mining the deformed

SAUNDERSFOOT, *The Harbour 1933* 85589

Pembrokeshire coal seams, saw a steady decline in the industry at Saundersfoot. The last colliery in the area closed in 1939. The same year the railway line also closed – it was taken up and sold as scrap iron after the outbreak of World War II. The final railway sleepers in Railway Street were taken up in 1955.

However, a new industry had already begun to develop, one that did not line the lungs with dust. From around 1870 there was an increasing interest in the area from seasonal visitors, and Saundersfoot began to emerge as a seaside resort, benefiting from the construction of a railway network through Wales. The impressive Victorian villas in the village reflect the attraction of Saundersfoot for well-to-do 19th-century society. With the decline of heavy industry, the harbour became a haven for pleasure cruising. By the turn of the 20th century, Saundersfoot was catering for its summer visitors with the provision of shops, hotels and lodging houses.

This growth coincided with a sense of community spirit enhanced by social gatherings such as sports, regattas and fairs.

World War II saw a lull in tourism. A full-scale rehearsal for the D-Day landings, Operation Jantzen, took place on the shore. Yet after the war, the village continued to develop. The noise of industry was a distant echo, although its remnants have become part of the local attractions. Thanks to the growing popularity of boating for leisure, Saundersfoot Sailing Club was formed in 1949. In 1952 the village became part of the Pembrokeshire Coast National Park, further encouraging holidaymakers to the area.

The natural beauty of the beaches, the tranquility of the village and the facilities provided for visitors made Saundersfoot a centre for an enjoyable family holiday. Tourism continues to sustain the village today and even through its developments it has lost none of the charm of a quaint seaside resort.

FRANCIS FRITH'S - TENBY AND SAUNDERSFOOT

TENBY: THE NORTH BAY

NORTH BEACH is a wide expanse of sand overlooking the harbour, with views across Carmarthen Bay. It is characterised by the large projecting rock halfway across the beach, and was the subject of one of the two surviving pictures of Tenby by J M W Turner in the 18th century, *The North Shore with Goscar Rock*.

FISHWIVES *1890* 28093
Posed on Goscar Rock on Tenby's North Beach, this group of women were paid for their work as models, and became the subject of many photographic portraits. Each day groups of these women from the village of Llangwm would walk 11 miles cross-country to Tenby to sell prawns, cockles and oysters, carried in their baskets and panniers.

TENBY: THE NORTH BAY

GENERAL VIEW
1890 28021

At the top of the cliff (right) stands an imposing house, Nyth-a-deryn, meaning 'bird's nest' or more commonly 'sparrow's nest'. It has a commanding view of the town and harbour. Below are Tenby luggers with their characteristic sails.

THE STEPS TO THE BEACH AND THE HARBOUR *1950* T23074

From 1892 this pathway and steps was known locally as 'Dead House Steps'. The path off to the left leads to the old town mortuary, located in a circular opening under the old fish market, which was built in 1847.

NORTH BAY 1950 T23076

The old smoke house (foreground) was built in 1848 in a romantic style to resemble an ancient castle, complete with mock stone cannons which aided the drainage from the private garden above. Inside, two great arches culminate in chimneys which project into the garden. However, there is no blackening of the ceiling, and indeed at the time of its completion local fishing was in decline.

GOSCAR ROCK 1925 77252

Here we see North Beach, with Goscar Rock surrounded by the retreating tide. The name Goscar is thought to be of Viking origin, and relates to its shape – 'ploughshare'. On the North Walk, visitors in their summer clothing which is very typical of the era.

TENBY: THE NORTH BAY

◀ **NORTH BEACH**
1950 T23071

In 1950, the majority of the visitors enjoying the beach in the height of the summer season would have been from Wales. The greatest concentration of people seems to be at the end of the North Walk, within close proximity to the two-storey building - the public lavatory - and beyond it the beach café (centre).

▶ **THE NORTH BAY**
1950 T23056

Above the cliffs we can just see the Park Hotel, built as a terrace of three houses, part of a larger development of North Cliff which never materialised. Formerly St Andrews School, during World War II the property was requisitioned for use by first British and then US troops. In 1950 it was divided into flats, but later, having fallen into a state of dereliction, it was converted into a hotel by the current owner's family.

TENBY: CASTLE HILL, CASTLE BEACH, ST CATHERINE'S ISLAND AND THE ESPLANADE

CASTLE HILL has a commanding view of both the landward and the seaward approaches, and it was almost certainly the location of an Iron Age Celtic promontory fort. Any archaeological evidence, however, has now been obliterated by Norman and later developments. The beaches, caves and rock pools around Castle Hill and especially St Catherine's Island have been a favourite haunt of the serious and amateur naturalist for generations. Above, the old fort, which has never fired a shot in anger, remains a reminder of the threat posed to Pembrokeshire by Napoleon III.

THE PIER AND THE HOTEL *1890* 24901

In the foreground we can see the roof of Laston House, a purpose-built bath-house which operated between 1810 and the early 1830s. Next door was the Assembly Rooms, which provided many elegant entertainments for wealthy visitors to Tenby. A glass and steel addition can be seen cantilevered from the back of the building, purposely built as the Excelsior Studios by photographer Charles Smith Allen.

TENBY: CASTLE HILL, CASTLE BEACH, ST CATHERINE'S ISLAND AND THE ESPLANADE

THE HARBOUR
c1960 T23152

The clear swathe below the Royal Lion Hotel (centre skyline) indicates the place where considerable work had to be undertaken after a landslide here claimed the lives of two young people who were crushed in a shelter on the North Walk in 1955. A crane can just be seen on the skyline above Goscar Rock (right) for the construction of Croft Court flats.

FROM CASTLE HILL *1925* 77264

A nursemaid sits with her two charges enjoying the sun on Castle Hill. Behind, a seating area nestles in the remnants of some ancient building whose purpose is now unclear. Today, the area is much hidden by flowers and shrubbery. Below (right) we can see the remains of the ancient wall defences of the castle.

THE CASTLE KEEP
1890 28084

Once a defender's last refuge, the Norman keep comprises a domed circular tower and square stair tower. Tenby has observed the weather for the Meteorological Office since 1892, and the tower still houses the sunshine meter. The shelter below the tower was also used for performances by the band. The statue is Wales's National Monument to Prince Albert, and was unveiled in 1865.

CASTLE HILL FROM THE BEACH 1890
28054

On the left is the Tenby Local Museum, which opened in 1878; it occupied the premises of the old National School building, and was established principally to house a valuable collection of geological specimens formerly belonging to the late Rev G N Smith. At the top of the hill is the old Coastguard House. It was built in about 1860, and is now privately owned.

SOUTH SANDS 1890 28049

The well-dressed ladies and children on the beach are most likely to be seasonal visitors to Tenby. The Victorians were avid collectors of many things, and the rocks, pools and caverns around St Catherine's Island were abundant with shells, ferns, various crustaceans, starfish, jellyfish and seaweed. The young man in the foreground has his foot upon a particularly large specimen.

TENBY: CASTLE HILL, CASTLE BEACH, ST CATHERINE'S ISLAND AND THE ESPLANADE

CASTLE SANDS
1925 77255

The booth at the top of the beach (right), in a place now occupied by Dennis's Café, reads 'Fancy Depot - Allen - Photographer'. It is thought that this booth was owned by 'Dai Photo', Bertram Edward Davies, who trained as a photographer under H Mortimer Allen. When Mortimer Allen died in 1926, Davies became the sole manager of the business.

SOUTH SANDS *c1925* T23004

Lexden Terrace (centre) was built in the Georgian style in 1843 by the builder and developer Captain John Rees. Shortly after its completion, Lexden House on the right was occupied by Rees's builder Mr Smith, and today it retains many of its original architectural features and details. The Sandygate lane leading to the beach was made possible by removing an old cottage between Cambrian House and St Julian's Terrace.

▶ ST CATHERINE'S ROCK
1890 28065

The War Office purchased the island in 1866 with a view to building a fort above South Sands, which was thought to be a likely landing place for the French at a time when there was a perceived threat from Napoleon III. The threat never materialised. 17 years after this picture was taken the island was sold to a private family.

TENBY: CASTLE HILL, CASTLE BEACH, ST CATHERINE'S ISLAND AND THE ESPLANADE

◀ **CASTLE HILL FROM ST CATHERINE'S ROCK**
1890 28052

A temporary bridge was erected from a ledge below the Store or Detachment Shelter on the left to Castle Hill, which allowed the passage of building materials and labourers from mainland to island at all states of the tide. Later the fort became known as one of Palmerston's follies owing to the surrender of Napoleon III in 1870 just a year after its completion.

THE FORT ON ST CATHERINE'S ROCK *1890* 28067

On the left is a landing stage or quay where we can just see a 2-ton crane. This lifting device was used during the construction of the fort to unload bulky building materials which could not be transported across to the island via the temporary bridge.

TENBY: CASTLE HILL, CASTLE BEACH, ST CATHERINE'S ISLAND AND THE ESPLANADE

ST CATHERINE'S ROCK
1890 28064

Advertisements on the Castle Beach bathing machines read 'Beecham's Pills save doctors bills', 'Beecham's Pills - worth a guinea a box' and 'Beecham's Pills - the key to health'. For the sake of modesty, bathing was not permitted on the beach without a machine, an expensive luxury at sixpence or a shilling, including towels; this tended to exclude less wealthy local people from their own beaches.

ST CATHERINE'S ROCK *1890* 28069

Traditionally in the ownership of wealthy occupants, the private steps leading down to the beach still belong to these houses, except those on the extreme left. The Iron Bar steps lead down the gully referred to as Breckmaenchine. Regarded as a defensive liability, it was fortified in about 1500 with a wall and towers, one of which can be seen overhung with ivy above the cliffs.

► SOUTH SHORE
c1960 T23102

From the sands it is possible to appreciate fully the outstanding position of the houses and hotels high on the Esplanade. The building with the round tower (centre) is the Imperial Hotel. In 1835 a tower, part of the town wall defences, was incorporated into what was then Belmont House; its height was increased by the addition of a turret to match the rest of the building.

TENBY: CASTLE HILL, CASTLE BEACH, ST CATHERINE'S ISLAND AND THE ESPLANADE

◀ **THE ESPLANADE**
The South Sands and St Catherine's Rock
c1925 T23006

The elegant row of houses on the left were part of a more extensive development of the land known as the Rope Walk Field; the plans were drawn up by the Council Surveyor in 1869. The Esplanade was a popular place for promenading, and here we see an attentive nursemaid with her pram-bound charge being admired by a passer-by.

FRANCIS FRITH'S - TENBY AND SAUNDERSFOOT

TENBY: INSIDE AND OUTSIDE THE WALLS

PROBABLY the best-known and most prominent feature of the walled town is the Five Arches, which date back to about 1328. This gateway, an innovative design brought back from the Crusades to the Holy Land, had its entrance on the side; this made it battering ram-proof, and brought invaders into the line of fire of defenders along the top of the wall. The original entrance has a slot for its portcullis, whereas the remaining four arches were knocked through in the 19th century to improve the flow of traffic in and out of the town. Tenby was never really designed for use by the motorcar, and apart from some Victorian road widening, with the demolition of some old terraces and properties, it still largely adheres to its medieval street system. Outside the town wall, many streets were laid out principally to provide lodging houses for the many visitors who came to the town once Tenby became part of the wider rail network.

THE OLD TOWN WALL c1950 T23002

This is St Florence Parade, with the Five Arches in the distance. The square gun tower on the right, c1500, was constructed against the curtain wall, and contains two chambers. The arrow slits are rounded at the bottom to accommodate early firearms and crossbows. Limerick or Belmont Arch was built in about 1865 to allow access to the Earl of Limerick's property on the other side of the wall.

TENBY: INSIDE AND OUTSIDE THE WALLS

THE TOWN WALLS
1893 28083

The South Pool Tower is rendered and more noticeably part of a dwelling, as it is still today. Beyond it, garages, long since demolished, were formally tenanted cottages. The decayed and demolished cottages on the left were also once tenanted; the area must have been already partly under construction as Southcliffe Gardens.

THE FIVE ARCHES *1890* 28078

Opposite the Five Arches were cottages built so closely that only a man walking or a horse being led could pass between them. Consequently, some 20 years before this photograph was taken, the Tenby Corporation enlarged an arch by knocking out the support, allowing carriages to pass into the town here. It is miraculous that the structurally weakened tower survived. The barrels to the left of the arch probably belong to the Bush Inn, whose cellar entrance can be seen between what were probably the naughty boys who cropped up regularly in local newspapers of the day. Although in 1882 the Great Western Electric Company felt themselves in a position to accept an application for the lighting of Tenby with electricity, the lamp on the arches (left) was probably gas.

THE WAR MEMORIAL, 1925 77271

The war memorial stands on a site formerly occupied by a stable, a coach house and two single-storey houses. It was formally opened by Lt Sackville Owen of the 1st Pembrokeshire Yeomanry in 1921 to commemorate 131 local men who perished in the Great War. More than 3000 local people witnessed the event, causing a reporter from the Tenby Observer to remark that this was a unique ceremony in the long history of the town, as it had never happened before and was unlikely to happen again.

THE CHURCH 1898 41062

Written records of St Mary's Church date back to 1210. The High Street is remarkably quiet, but it is captured at a time of largely horse-drawn transport. Tuckers Haircutting Rooms (right), next to the bank, have an advertising lantern; on the left, the first property is Jasperly House, now Boots the Chemist, but at the time of the photograph a wine merchant's belonging to Philip G Harris.

YE OLDE GIFTE SHOPPE
c1965 T23163

This is the oldest surviving shop front in Tenby (left); shoppers are required to step down into these premises. Next door is W Howells the jeweller, and then comes the Bush Inn, which dates back to c1860 – it was formerly a blacksmith's shop. Beyond is the South West Gate or Five Arches. The Welcome Café, now Fecci's Ice Cream Parlour, is opposite, and on either side of it are D A Sutherland and a draper's and men's outfitter's, which are now gift shops.

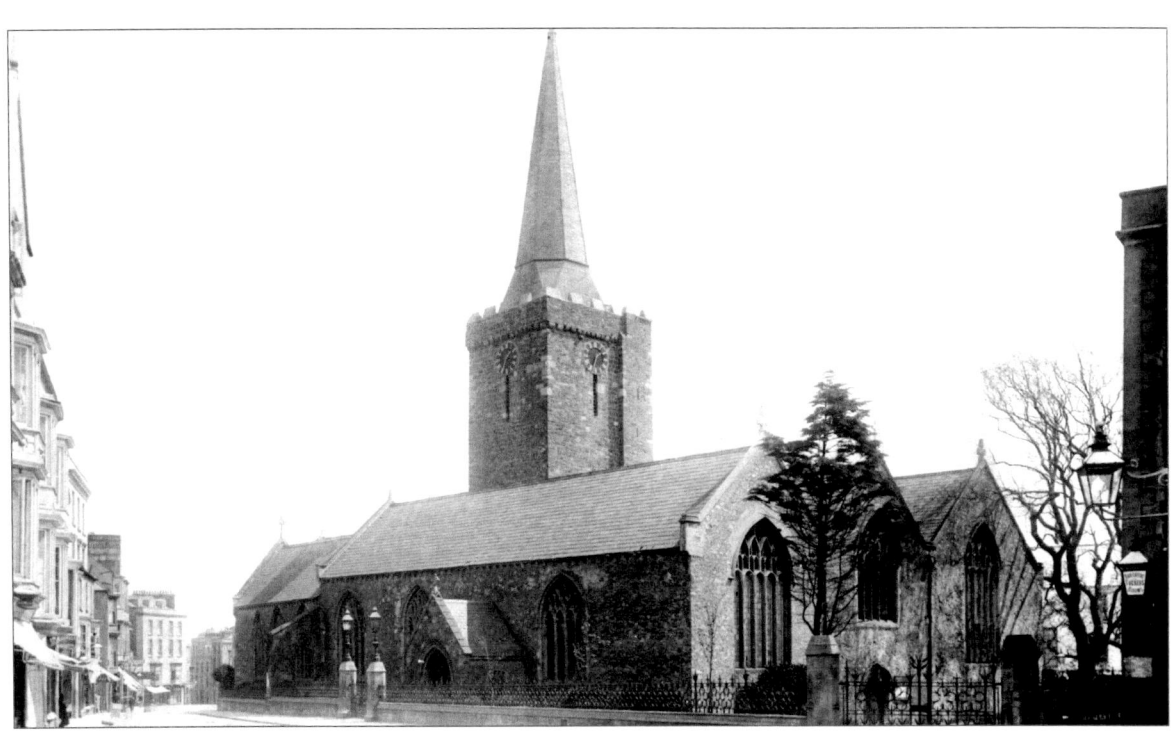

TENBY: INSIDE AND OUTSIDE THE WALLS

◀ **THE CEMETERY**
1890 28090

When in 1853 the population of Tenby had reached 3000, it was decided that a new cemetery and chapel should be constructed on the outskirts of the town on the Lower Windmill Field. A tender for the work amounted to £508. The chapel bell, which cost a further £33 3s, was cast in 1855 from the same batch of metal as Big Ben.

TENBY: INSIDE AND OUTSIDE THE WALLS

THE PARISH CHURCH
1890 24920

The spire of St Mary's Church rises to 152 feet, and is a landmark for miles around. The drinking fountain in the middle of Tudor Square was erected by the Mayor, Dr Frederick Dyster, in 1867 to commemorate Lieutenant Colonel Thomas Wedgwood, who fought at Waterloo. To the left is the Manchester Warehouse, 'complete house furnishers'. The heavily laden coach appears to serve either the Royal Gatehouse or the Lion Hotel.

HIGH STREET
1950 T23058

Sixty years after No 24920 was taken, the proliferation of the motor vehicle occupying the kerbs is noticeable. The Bay Tree Café (left) survives today, and so does T P Hughes & Son (at the furthest visible end of the High Street), established in 1902. On the right, amongst the premises visible are Cash & Co, a shoe shop, Olivers Shoes, Lloyds Bank, and one of Tenby's oldest shops, Medical Hall, established in the 1830s. The post office is clearly identifiable from the telegraph wires on its roof; it relocated to this site in 1858. In 1950 Mr W J Griffiths was postmaster. In 1962 it moved to Warren Street.

TENBY: THE HARBOUR

IN 1328, during Edward III's reign, rights were given to 'the good men of Tenby' so that the town might benefit from taxes of murage and lastage applied to goods coming into the town by sea. With the money raised by these taxes, the townsfolk should maintain the walls of the town and build a pier to defend the harbour, and it is thought that Tenby had the earliest pier in Wales. Fishing and especially dredging for oysters was an important part of Tenby's trade. Oysters from the Caldey beds were so large that a single specimen was considered too much for one person. However, over many years and with a decline in the availability of oysters, and subsequently an increasing dependency on the new industry catering for seasonal visitors, the importance of fishing in Tenby lessened. Fishermen came from elsewhere around the coast, and soon Brixham trawlers became a common sight in the harbour. They would berth amongst the shallow-drafted clinker-built Tenby luggers peculiar to the town, three-masted open boats used mainly for drift-net fishing and oyster dredging. Throughout the 19th century, luggers were still built in Tenby. In summer, many luggers provided pleasure trips for visitors, a more profitable trade than fishing.

THE HARBOUR *1898* 41065

The 200-foot Royal Victoria Pier (left) was built out from Castle Hill at Butlers Horse, and was erected to coincide with Queen Victoria's Jubilee in 1897. In 1898 work was being undertaken to extend it further. This was completed in 1899, and opened on 9 May by the Duchess of Kent. A popular promenade, it was also used as a low water landing stage for excursions and paddle steamers. It was demolished in 1953.

TENBY: THE HARBOUR

CASTLE HILL
c1950 T23024

After 50 years of manual launching, which required horses and at least 50 men to haul the lifeboat into the water and could take more than an hour to achieve, the lifeboat house and slip was built close to Royal Victoria Pier in 1905. The building cost £3,871 19s 2d, but also, tragically, the life of Joseph Banham, who whilst working fell 50 feet, sustaining fatal injuries.

THE HARBOUR *1950* T23075

The low building on the pier was home to the RAF Marine Branch. During World War II marine craft were engaged in anti-submarine work and the defence of the western approaches. From 1940-47, No 48 Air Sea Rescue Unit was based here. After the war, marine craft in Tenby were chiefly employed in providing Range Safety in Carmarthen Bay. The RAF Marine Branch closed in 1985.

TENBY: THE HARBOUR

THE HARBOUR
1950 T23061

Now the Tenby Sailing Club, the large building on the left is the former Sleeman Stores; built in the 18th century, it stood on piers, spanning the sluice. The Sleeman family imported a variety of goods, including wine, vinegar and fruits. Two members of the Sleeman family are remembered in St Mary's Church as being instrumentally involved in eradicating the cult of Thuggee in India during the early part of the 19th century. The large boat in the foreground is the *Janwal*, owned by Jimmy R Crockford.

▼ THE HARBOUR 1950 T23063

The pier is busy with sightseers and people returning from excursions to Caldey Island. Among the boats moored are Mr Walter Bushell's *Eureka* and *Monty* owned by Mr Jimmy John. The bollards are purpose-built. Further along the pier, performing the same function are embedded cannons dating from the 17th and 19th centuries. The large boat moored along side the pier wall is the RAF boat.

▶ THE HARBOUR 1950 T23062

Amongst the boats in the harbour are *Victoria*, *Kestrel*, *Primrose* and *Foam*. *Foam* was one of the last boats to be built in Tenby by Gorgy Wickland, who used the old lifeboat house on Castle Sands as his workshop. All these boats had Kelvin engines using a petrol/paraffin fuel mix. Built for only £60, *Foam* was designed to carry 12 passengers to Caldey.

TENBY: THE HARBOUR

◀ **THE HARBOUR**
1890 28041

The girl carrying a baby (left) and the children playing in the boats are noticeably not visitors. Rooted here by their connection with the sea, the people living in the harbour were a separate population from the rest of the town, and a visitor to Tenby noted that 'in town boys are limited to their mischief but at the seaside they command another element and keep you in a state of nervous fever'. On the shore, registered M26, is *Annie*, a 23-ton trawling ketch with a 45ft keel; owned by George Rowe of Harding Street, it carried 2 men and a boy. Behind is a Tenby lugger; in 1891 there were 49 in use.

▶ **THE HARBOUR WALL**
1950 T23067

A boy stands on the old slipway into the sluice. At high tide the basin would fill; it was then emptied through an opening at the other end, keeping the harbour free of silt. A number of people have gathered on the Mayor's Slip, named in honour of Alderman Clement Williams, Mayor of Tenby in 1901 and 1904.

CALDEY

CALDEY ISLAND is 1½ miles long and ½ mile wide, and lies 3 miles distant from Tenby; it takes only 20 minutes to reach the island in one of the Caldey Pool boats. The name Caldey derives from 'Keld Eye', meaning 'cold island', a name given by its Viking visitors between the 10th and 11th centuries. Its Welsh name is Ynys Pyr, referring to the first abbot of the monastic settlement, which dates back to the 6th century. In 1136 Caldey Island became the property of the Benedictine monks from the abbey of Tiron in France, and in part, ancient buildings dating back to about this time still stand. Today, having gone through many hands and changes, Caldey is home to a community of Reformed Cistercian monks.

THE SLIPWAY *c1965* C373020

The first reference to a slipway on Priory Bay was in 1897. In 1958, owing to increases in the amount of farm produce being transported from Caldey, steps were taken to improve the landing facility for boats. Redundant barges, relics from the D-Day landings, were filled with concrete and sunk to extend the slipway. Landing alongside, a boat from Tenby is collecting waiting day visitors to the island.

THE CALVARY
c1960 C373026

Above Priory Bay at the top of the Fuchsia Steps, the Caldey Calvary was erected by the Cistercian monks of the island in 1945. The cross and figure of Christ are carved in wood. Attached is an inscription which reads:

'Wanderer stay still and think

On me here a little while

How I hung on the cross, so

That thou should come to me.'

THE ABBEY *c1960* C373047

The monastery was designed by the architect Coates Carter and completed between 1910 and 1913. Its red tiled roofs and whitewashed walls are clearly visible from Tenby, 3 miles away on the mainland. In the foreground are a row of workmen's cottages built in about 1910, and on the right is the post office, which now houses the island's museum.

THE PRIORY CHURCH
c1965 C373040

This is the old priory and church dedicated to St Illtud - its leaning spire is clearly visible. The building in front of the spire was part of a mansion belonging to a former owner of the island; it was finally demolished in the 1970s as a result of serious storm damage some years earlier. In the foreground is the priory fishpond.

◄ **THE LIGHTHOUSE** *c1960* C373041

Built in 1829 at Chapel Point on the southern end of Caldey Island by Joseph Nelson, the light stands 210 feet above the high water mark. The lighthouse remains the property of Trinity House, but the keepers' cottages are now in the ownership of the religious community.

FRANCIS FRITH'S - TENBY AND SAUNDERSFOOT

SAUNDERSFOOT

COMPOSITE POSTCARD *c1965* S64245

This composite card was intended to attract visitors of all ages by showing the facilities of the village, including the long stretches of popular beaches with safe bathing, and the enticing promise of a pleasure cruise from its picturesque harbour. Tourism is the industry that has sustained Saundersfoot since the closing of the last colliery in 1939.

SAUNDERSFOOT

THE VIEW FROM GRIFFITHSTON HILL
1898 41072

One side of High Street is not fully developed at this date. The building in the centre of the picture is Evelyn Coffee Tavern, opened in 1885 by Lady Evelyn Campbell using public money. It was designed to offer alternative refreshments to the public houses. It later accommodated the magistrate's court. Brewery Meadow, the undeveloped land behind Milford Street, was one of the sites for the annual Danter's Fair.

ST BRIDE'S *1906* 53903
The mother and child appear to have been dressed and posed especially for the photograph. In late Victorian and early Edwardian times, this part of the village was regarded as a select residential area. The turning to the right off St Bride's Hill leads down to the Glen. The fields have now been more fully developed with residential property.

▼ THE GLEN 1934 86455a

This view of the Glen was taken from St Bride's Hill. It is possible to reach the Glen Beach from just below the row of houses. The houses in the picture still remain, but some are extended and altered, and they are now surrounded by newer residential properties. Rhode Wood, accessible from the Glen, offers many pleasant sylvan walks.

► ST BRIDE'S
1925 77274

Here we view Swallowtree Cove (known also as Swallowtree Dip or Washfield Lake) and the Glen Beach, or Dingle Beach, from Swallowtree Woods. The rock in the centre of the picture is the Lady Cave anticline. This famous geological fold shows the intense deformity of the rock formation of the coalfield. The beach directly to the west side of the harbour is Back Beach.

SAUNDERSFOOT

◄ **GENERAL VIEW**
c1955 S64049

This view of the village was taken from St Bride's. The Square, the building located at the head of the slipway, was once the village post office and is now part of the Mermaid restaurant. The car park, previously the village green, was laid in the mid 1950s under Lord Merthyr's authority.

► **ST BRIDE'S HOTEL**
Composite Postcard
c1955 S64092

This postcard, probably used for advertising purposes, shows views of and from St Bride's Hotel, with its commanding position over Carmarthen Bay. At this time the hotel offered numerous facilities, including 50 bedrooms, bedside lights in all rooms, electric fires in first-floor rooms, a tennis court, a putting green, television, a ladies' hairdressing saloon and a private path to the beach, which is no longer available today.

▼ **ST BRIDE'S HOTEL** *c1955* S64126

St Bride's Hotel was built on the site of an old white house where previously a farm had stood. Originally called the Carrington, St Bride's Hotel was requisitioned by the Admiralty during World War II and became the Royal Marines School of Signalling until after VJ-Day.

▶ **FROM ST BRIDE'S**
1933 85581

Here we have a panoramic view of the stretch of shoreline at Saundersfoot from Front Beach to Coppet Hall – Coppet Hill and Coppet Hall Point are at the far end of the beach. The patch of grass behind was the village green, later converted into a car park. Note also the steam crane on the harbour (right).

SAUNDERSFOOT

◀ **CAMBRIAN TERRACE** *1949*
S64044

The Cambrian Hotel (left) stood on the site which had housed the Milford Arms since 1680 – it was renamed in 1870. The terrace was built c1865. The Hean Castle Hotel (centre) stands on the corner of Cambrian Terrace and Wogan Terrace. On the right is the Barbecue restaurant, originally Bonville's Court Colliery Office. Following a fire in 1913, the building was reconstructed. It is now the Tourist Information Centre.

▶ **THE HARBOUR**
1925 77280

This is the south quay of the harbour. The harbour was built between 1829 and 1834 from local and imported stone. When Bonville's Court Colliery opened, the harbour was used for exporting coal; between 1912 and 1926 the colliery produced more than 35,000 tonnes of anthracite annually. On the harbour is a steam crane that provided assistance for unloading cargo, operated for many years by Ben Lewis.

FRANCIS FRITH'S - TENBY AND SAUNDERSFOOT

THE HARBOUR
1933 85587

The boat with the wide stripe and symmetrical ends (centre) is a large old lifeboat. Formerly this vessel would have required a team of brave men to row her to those in distress on the sea. By 1933 it would probably have been converted by having an engine fitted, and would most likely have been used for pleasure trips around the coast.

THE HARBOUR *1933* 85589

At the far side of the harbour (left) we can just see a row of approximately ten coal trolleys that have brought their load to the harbour ready for shipping. On the wall are two bays with their gear for loading the boats which transported the coal from Saundersfoot to places of industry elsewhere.

SAUNDERSFOOT

THE HARBOUR *c1955* S64243

The large boat SA113 alongside the pier is a fishing trawler from Swansea. Wearing his flat cap and standing on the smaller craft, the *Victoria* built by Gorgy Wickland, is Billy Richards. This was the only boat in Saundersfoot able to take visitors to Caldey Island.

THE HARBOUR
c1965 S64103

The exporting of coal has ceased by this date, and the loading gear and coal trolleys are long gone. At the base of the cliff, the buildings include the one belonging to the boat builders Kelpie Boat Services. They employed several local men, including James and Charles Crockford, and here boats like the *Nemesis* and the *Polar Star* were built. Kelpie Boat Services still operates, but is nowadays located in Pembroke Dock.

THE PROMENADE AND THE BEACH
1949 S64039

The promenade along the harbour gave tourists the opportunity to take a refreshing walk along the seafront. Six years before this picture was taken, the beaches at Saundersfoot witnessed secret military activity with Operation Jantzen, the full-scale rehearsals for the D-Day landings. The building on the corner is now part of the Mermaid restaurant.

SAUNDERSFOOT

▲ **HIGH STREET** *1949* S64038

The large white building is the Hean Castle Hotel, previously the Picton Castle Hotel, and still a popular hostelry in the village. George Borrow, author of *Wild Wales*, stayed here in 1857. The Castle Stores (right) was owned by Thomas McLoughlin, brother of Harry who owned the motor and cycle depot, and supplied such temptations as 'fresh fruit, vegetables, sweetmeats, soda fountain and delicious ices'.

◄ **RAILWAY STREET** *1949* S64037

Railway Street was renamed The Strand in 1950. The garage (left) was owned by Harry McLoughlin, and offered lock-up garage accommodation as well as accessories for the motorist. Railway Street, built from ballast dumped on the beach from coal ships, was so named because the inland coalmines were connected to the harbour by railway lines which ran along the street.

FRANCIS FRITH'S - TENBY AND SAUNDERSFOOT

SAUNDERSFOOT

THE BEACH
1933 85582

This view shows Front Beach and Railway Street, now the Strand. In the foreground is Craig-y-Mor or Rock Villa. The small building in the garden was originally a boathouse. Just beyond the house, at the furthest east end of the street, is the railway tunnel that connects Saundersfoot with Coppet Hall. Properties on the seaward side are almost unique in Britain, as they front onto the beach without a road between.

COPPET HALL SANDS
c1955 S64154

We are looking from Coppet Hall Point. The people to the right are enjoying a walk along the miner's route of the Stepaside line, which transported anthracite from the Stepaside area via Wiseman's Bridge, first by horse-drawn trams and afterwards by rail.

COPPET HALL
1898 41076

A group of children pose for the photograph. Coppet Hall's name is believed to be derived from 'coal pit haul': before the laying of the railway track in the 1870s, a tramline existed on which coal was hauled on horse-drawn trucks to the beach to be loaded onto waiting boats. A coal wagon (far right) stands upon the old line adjoining the track.

SAUNDERSFOOT

▲ **HEAN CASTLE** *1898* 41075

Situated on the outskirts of Saundersfoot, Hean Castle (its name is probably derived from the Welsh Yr Hen Castell, meaning 'the old castle') is part of an estate that benefited from the prosperity of the industrial period. Charles Ranken Vickerman acquired the house in 1860, reconstructing it in 1876 into a crenellated Victorian residence, and building it in the red sandstone which had come in as ballast on the boats.

◀ **ST ISSELL'S CHURCH** *1898* 41077

Parts of St Issell's parish church date back to Norman times. Later additions include the 13th-century tower and chancel arch, and the north aisle and the arch in the north choir from the 14th century. Under F R Kempson of Llandaff and Hereford, the church was restored and extended in 1864. The building in the grounds housed St Issell's National School. In 1856 a 2-acre cemetery was provided for the parish at a cost of £700.

FRANCIS FRITH'S - TENBY AND SAUNDERSFOOT

AMROTH AND WISEMAN'S BRIDGE

AMROTH AND WISEMAN'S BRIDGE lie east of Saundersfoot. An earthen mound was located south of today's Amroth church, a form of rath or prehistoric fort, situated to defend any approach from the sea through the valley. There was a vast stretch of moorland in Amroth during medieval times, as well as areas of cultivated land, including the parishettes of Merrixton and Earweare. There was also much forestry in the area, and today at low tide remnants of a sunken forest can be seen on Amroth's shore. There is also evidence of a Roman villa at Trelissey. Today, Amroth is a small seaside village from where the Pembrokeshire Coast Path begins.

Iron ore was dug between Amroth and Wiseman's Bridge, and during Saundersfoot's industrial age it was exported. A brickworks also opened at Woodside, between Hean Castle and Wiseman's Bridge, in about 1845. Today the hamlet of Wiseman's Bridge lies within the parish of St Issell.

AMROTH, *Composite Postcard c1965* A187083

Built on the site of an earlier Norman castle at the turn of the 19th century, Amroth Castle (centre) hosted a lunch in 1802 for Nelson and Sir William and Lady Emma Hamilton when they visited the county. Today the cows are gone, and the castle and grounds have become a hotel and caravan park.

◀ **AMROTH**
The Amroth Arms c1965 A187054

The land in front of the Amroth Arms which extended eastwards to the Castle gate was formerly known by local people as Croggan's Cliff. 'Croggans' is a local name for the Welsh-speaking holidaymakers and visitors.

AMROTH AND WISEMAN'S BRIDGE

◄ **AMROTH**
The Beach c1960
A187048

Amroth is a former coal mining village at the southerly end of the 186 mile-long Pembrokeshire Coast Path. The groynes on the beach indicate the ferocious tidal currents; in 1931 these currents seriously undermined a row of cottages up the road on the seaward side, that were subsequently swept away. Immediately in the left foreground once stood a stable with a bandstand above.

▲ **WISEMAN'S BRIDGE,** *The Wiseman's Bridge Inn c1965* S64189

This settlement probably got its name from Andrew Wysmon, a tenant knight at the time of Edward II's reign. The large extension at the back of the inn (right) contained seven bedrooms with doors onto the beach. During the Second World War the beach was used by troops preparing for the D-Day landings, and Winston Churchill enjoyed a cup of tea at the inn.

◄ **WISEMAN'S BRIDGE**
The Village c1965
A187062

The inn (centre) has grown over the years to encompass two cottages plus additions to provide holiday accommodation and a restaurant. The inn has been in the possession of the Kemble family since 1956. Disaster struck on Christmas Eve 2002 when fire gutted much of the building. Fortunately, the old bar escaped fire damage; the inn was rebuilt, and reopened on 12 December 2003.

FRANCIS FRITH'S - TENBY AND SAUNDERSFOOT

CLIFFS, CAVES AND COVES

THE PEMBROKESHIRE coastline is dramatic and beautiful, and its geological features have been popular with holiday makers over the centuries. An excursion to experience the coastal splendour first hand would have been a common activity for those interested in the natural world, and various modes of transport would have been employed to get there: boat, train, charabanc, cart or carriage, and, of course, on foot. In order to avoid being cut off by the rising tide, walkers making their way from Tenby to Lydstep Cavern Beach were being advised to depart for their destination two hours before low tide.

LYDSTEP, *The Cliffs 1890* 28005
This is the westerly end of Lydstep Cavern Beach; here we see the aptly named Saddle Back and Saddle Point, with the cave and fissures worn into the vertical strata of limestone.

CLIFFS, CAVES AND COVES

LYDSTEP, *Cave of Beauty 1890* 28006
The 'Droch' or Cave of Beauty is regarded as the finest at Lydstep Cavern Beach. It has a smaller secondary entrance as well as the magnificent opening seen here, where two well-dressed couples stand. Abundant with a variety of ferns including sea spleenwort, this beach became a most popular excursion from Tenby.

LYDSTEP
Smuggler's Cave
1890 28007

This is a tunnel cavern, with a large natural skylight and both landward and coastal entrances. The Lydstep caverns are only accessible at low tide, with the exception of the Smuggler's Cave, which was probably so named because of the high incidence of smuggling along the rocky coastline of Pembrokeshire - particularly in isolated bays where contraband could be stored.

LYDSTEP
The Bay 1890 28016A

Lydstep Point lies to the west, with the headland ravaged by the effects of quarrying limestone. Lydstep Haven is today, as then, privately owned, but now the gentle slopes down towards the beach are covered with caravans.

CLIFFS, CAVES AND COVES

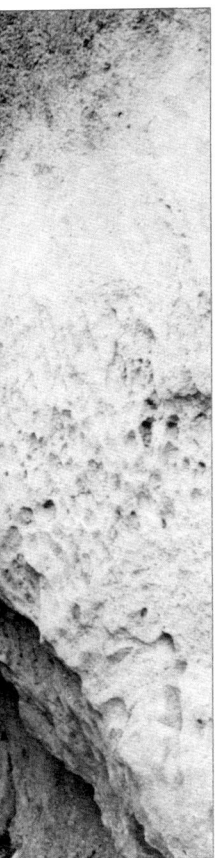

▲ **LYDSTEP,** *Caldey Island 1890* 28019A

The boy in the foreground is looking through his telescope, possibly at passing shipping but more probably at Lundy Island. From Tenby, Lundy is obscured by Caldey Island (which we see here off shore), but beyond lies Lundy, some 25 miles off and clearly visible on a clear day, rising 400 feet up out of the Bristol Channel.

◄ **GILTAR POINT AND THE SANDS**
c1955 P23021

Giltar Point is an expanse of limestone projecting out into the sea at the end of Tenby's South Beach. Popular with walkers, it has always been noted for its exceptional views and for the abundance of wild flowers.

MONKSTONE POINT *1890* 28111

In the distance is Monkstone Point, so called because of the remains of a monastic cell which were discovered among the precipitous rocks there. Long before the establishment of the Pembrokeshire Coast Path, a well-worn track can clearly be seen winding its way around the headland.

CLIFFS, CAVES AND COVES

MONKSTONE POINT
The Rocks 1890 28116

Accessible only at low tide, these barnacle-covered rocks at Monkstone Point are comprised largely of millstone grits, with evidence of the Coal Measures and considerable geological movement. Monkstone is itself a weathered but compound anticline.

THE STACKS *1890* 24926
Also known as the Flimston or Elegug Stacks (Elegug is derived from the Welsh word for guillemot), these two massive pillars are comprised of limestone. Under constant assault from the sea, the geology of Pembrokeshire has produced some of the finest coastal scenery in Britain.

THE CASTLES OF CAREW AND MANORBIER

THE CASTLES OF CAREW AND MANORBIER

CAREW CASTLE began its life as a Norman stronghold, but archaeological evidence suggests that there was an even earlier Celtic fort here. This was clearly an important site, and possibly a royal residence of the earlier powerful Welsh dynasties; evidence for this is the presence of one of the finest Celtic crosses in Wales. The castle has undergone many changes over the years. The most recent significant addition is the north range, built at a time when Carew was being converted into a comfortable Elizabethan mansion.

The small village of Manorbier is only five miles distant from Tenby, lying in the valley of a west-facing bay. Originally the castle was more a fortified manor house, and the name of the subsequent town and castle almost certainly derive from the Welsh 'Maenor Pyr', meaning 'a holding of land in the ownership of Pyro' – Pyro was the first abbot of Caldey Island in the 6th century. Manorbier was the birthplace in c1145 of one of Wales's most interesting churchmen, Giraldus Cambrensis or Gerallt O Gymru; he thought Manorbier one of the most pleasant places in the country.

CAREW CASTLE AND THE BRIDGE *c1960* C24001
Beyond the castle is the tidal mill; it is set on a causeway which dams the Carew River, forming this 23-acre mill-pond. Although there has been a mill on the site since 1542, the present building dates to the 19th century, and was operational until 1937. The view has changed very little today, except for the development of the cottage next to the bridge, the Riverside Restaurant.

► CAREW CASTLE FROM THE NORTH WEST
1893 32816

The west range of the castle to the right dates back to the 13th century, whereas the heavily fenestrated north range to the left is Elizabethan, the work of Sir John Perrot, half-brother of Elizabeth I. The glazing of the many paned windows and impressive oriels was never completed, thanks to Perrot's unfortunate incarceration in the Tower of London.

◄ CAREW CASTLE
The Celtic Cross
c1960 C24009

An inscription on the west face of Carew's Celtic cross commemorates Maredudd ap Edwin, joint ruler of the kingdom of Deheubarth in south west Wales, who died two years into his reign in 1035. Today the wall behind the cross has been removed to improve the view of both cross and Carew Castle beyond.

THE CASTLES OF CAREW AND MANORBIER

▲ **MANORBIER,** *The Castle and the Village 1890* 27980

This clearly shows the castle and the few buildings of the old village as being set in a steep-sided valley. On the left is St James' church with its Norman tower, which dates back to the 12th century; on the right a small round tower is the remains of a dovecote which once stood close to the castle fishpond.

◀ **MANORBIER**
The Castle 1890 27981

The castle was erected on a red sandstone spur from locally quarried limestone. It occupies an excellent defensive position overlooking the sea and the beach beyond, where Giraldus Cambrensis played as child. In 1890 it would appear that fields immediately next to the castle were grazed, whereas today the fields to the right and foreground around the castle are covered with trees, bushes and undergrowth.

MANORBIER, *The Castle, the Gate and the Drawbridge 1890* 27985
The gatehouse was built in the 13th century, and it is situated next to some of the earliest stone structures in the castle: the Old Tower on the right was built in the 12th century, and a fighting gallery and curtain wall to the left were built in about 1230. The chains are attached to a wooden drawbridge spanning a ditch, but these are a more recent addition.

MANORBIER, *The Castle c1955* M24034

The four-storey round tower in the distance at the south-east angle, strongly built, remains today in perhaps the best state of preservation of all the castle buildings. When the castle was under siege, one might have expected many men to be stationed here, yet there are no hearths or latrines. The large chimney on the guardroom (centre) is of a style attributed to the Flemings, who arrived with the Normans.

FRANCIS FRITH'S - TENBY AND SAUNDERSFOOT

MANORBIER
The Castle c1960
M24062

Looking from the southern headland back towards the castle, one can imagine the mill pond that existed in Giraldus Cambrensis' time located in the flat area to the right of the castle; in this photograph the area is occupied by caravans, and today it is a car park. In days gone by smuggling was rife, and Manorbier Castle is rumoured to have tunnels and hiding places for contraband.

THE BURROWS, GUMFRESTON AND PENALLY

THE BURROWS is a large expanse of sand dunes and drift that has built up over the years, and significantly so since the railway line was laid across what was formerly a fairly extensive estuary of the River Ritec. Beyond lies Penally, with its quaint church dedicated to one of the most famous Welsh saints, Teilo, who was born here. Gumfreston lies on a raised hill between two arms of the estuary, and was once accessible by sea by boats making their way up river.

PENALLY, *The Burrows 1890* 28099
We are looking from the Tenby side of the dunes to Penally in the middle distance. These dunes built up from about 1820 onwards. Eventually, in 1863, after successive attempts to build an embankment across the marshland and the estuary of the River Ritec to halt flooding of this low-lying land, the Tenby Pembroke Railway line was laid using the foundations of an earlier embankment.

THE BURROWS, GUMFRESTON AND PENALLY

TENBY
*From the Burrows
1893* 32804

The arches upon which the Esplanade roadway was constructed are clearly visible. During World War II the Burrows were heavily mined and covered with barbed wire, and even today at some very low tides it is still possible to see old metal bars or rails that were laid down to prevent aircraft landing on the beach.

TENBY, *From the Burrows 1925* 77269
Here we see the Black Rock, Black Rock Quarry and Black Rock Cottage, and behind is the bridge over the railway. Originally there was a junction here with a line running to the original Tenby Station, now Tenby Lower Yard; from that line a short spur served the quarry and lime kilns. The quarry ceased to be worked in 1911.

GUMFRESTON
The Water Mill 1890
28104

'Cawson' (Causeway) Mill on Gumfreston Hill is today only a ruin. But this tranquil scene with a woman and girls in what appears to be their Sunday best (left), and the young lad fishing in the mill pond (top right), belies an unpleasant incident which took place near here in 1839 when a duel was fought between Mayor William Richards and Henry Mannix, a knight's son.

GUMFRESTON, *Scotsborough Lane 1890* 28108
In the distance are the ruins of a once great mansion, Scotsborough, dating back to the 14th century. It passed through a variety of hands and was last occupied in 1824, when it was converted to tenements. An epidemic of smallpox broke out amongst the inhabitants, and the survivors then fled the house. Despite their decay, the ruins still display some fine architectural details.

GUMFRESTON, *The Church 1890* 28101

The church is dedicated to St Lawrence. The nave and chancel date back to the 12th century; the tower is 13th century. Gumfreston is famous for its healing chalybeate wells, which were visited by pilgrims making their way to St David's, and there was probably a Celtic church of significance here prior to the coming of the Normans. Contemporary pilgrims here may witness the revived tradition of well dressing.

PENALLY
*The Round Tower
1890* 28098

Originally arranged on two floors, the tower dates back to medieval times, but its purpose remains something of a mystery. It has been suggested that it served as a beacon, as a watch tower and more latterly as a snuff mill. It is popular with sightseers - the resting walker gives scale to the building. It now stands in a cottage garden overlooking Black Rock Quarry.

PENALLY, *The View towards Tenby 1890* 28094

The 16th-century tower of the church of St Nicholas and St Teilo rises above the rooftops of leafy Penally. The tree line follows the line of the Tenby Pembroke railway track. The white building in the middle ground is Crossing Cottage; beyond are the gentle slopes of the burrows and Tenby golf course, the oldest links course in Wales, established in 1888.

INDEX

SAUNDERSFOOT

Amroth 66-67
Beach 60-61
Cambrian Terrace 54-55
Composite Postcard 50, 65
Coppet Hall 62
Coppet Hall Sands 62-63
General View 52-53
Harbour 55, 56, 57, 58-59
Hean Castle 63
High Street 59
Promenade and the Beach 58
Railway Street 59
St Brides 51, 52, 54
St Bride's Hotel 53, 54
St Issell's Church 63
The Glen 52
View from Griffithston Hill 51
Wisemans Bridge 67

TENBY

Castle Hill 41
Castle Hill from St Catherine's
Castle Hill from the Beach 24

Castle Keep 22-23
Castle Sands 25
Cemetery 34
Church 35
Esplanade 30-31
Fishwives 16
Five Arches 33
Fort on St Catherine's Rock 28, 29
From Castle Hill 21
General View 17
Goscar Rock 18
Harbour 17
Harbour 21, 40, 41, 42-43, 44-45
Harbour Wall 45
High Street 38-39
North Bay 18, 19
North Beach 18-19
Old Town Wall 32
Parish Church 36-37
Pier and the Hotel 20
St Catherine's Rock 26-27
South Sands 24, 25
South Shore 30-31
Steps to the Beach and the Harbour

17
Town Walls 33
War Memorial 34
Ye Olde Gifte Shoppe 34-35

CALDEY

Abbey 48
Carew Castle 76
Carew Castle and the Bridge 75
Carew Castle from the
Giltar Point and the Sands 71
Gumfreston 84-85, 86, 87
Lighthouse 49
Lydstep 68, 69, 70-71
Manorbier 77, 78, 79, 80-81
Monkstone Point 72, 73
North West Cliffs 76-77
Penally 82, 88
Priory Church 48-49
Slipway 46-47
Tenby 83
The Calvary 48
The Stacks 73

NAMES OF SUBSCRIBERS

The following people have kindly supported this book
by subscribing to copies before publication.

Tony Allen on his 60th Birthday

Ms Elaine Sue, James and Emma Allen, Reynalton

Jenny Archer

Jennifer A. Ballinger

Mr & Mrs J. Barrow, Tenby

The Beynon Family, Saundersfoot

Mr D. R. Bolton & Mrs L. D. Bolton, Tenby

In Memory of Harry (Blackie) Bolton, Tenby

Perry 'Co' Bowen

Alun 'Big Al' Bowen

Ruth Brace, St Florence

John & Elsie Brady, Liverpool

Christine Elizabeth Brown

Colin Alan Burke, Harries Street

Cattini Family, Caldey Island

Paul Cavill, Gloucester

In Memory of B. Clark, Sale, Cheshire

N. J. Clark, Amroth

Bill & Beryl Conway

D. Ken Daniels, Saundersfoot

In Memory of Ena Davies, Tenby P.O., 1942

Love to my favourite sister Gwen Davies & Family

Ken & Ena (nee Lovering) Davies, Golden 6/2/04

With love to Shirley & Kerry Davies

With love to my brother Trevor Davies & Family

For his christening William Trefor Davies

Mr J. & Mrs V. Donohue, Sale, Cheshire

Mr & Mrs A. T. Dowler, Saundersfoot

Mr Ray Duffy, Tenby

Richard B. Eastlake

William Edwards

John & Maureen Egginton, Begelly

Margaret Peggy Ellen, Silverwood

Gerald Evans, (formerly) Five Arches, Tenby

John Evans, Old Coastguard House

Shirley Ford-Pucknell

The Gardner Family, Tenby, Pembrokeshire

The Gray Family of Wednesfield

Les & Gwen Grecian

With love to Greg and Moira

Wyn I. Griffiths, Tenby

Mr D. L. & Mrs G. C. Haddrell, Worcester

The Hart Family, Saundersfoot

Arthur, Connie, Cecil, Alan, Neville, Alec Hart

Peter & Alyson Hicks, Kilgetty

Sydney John Ible, Chester

Michele Iles

Mr R. E. & Mrs M. F. James, Studley

The Johnson Family, Herts

Anne Jones

In Memory of Beatrice Yvonne Jones

Elaine Jones-Evans & Peter Evans, 2004

Mr G. A. & Mrs R. E. Jones, Cardiff

Janet 'Gerbals' Jones

Mr & Mrs J. Keohane and Family, Penally

Chrissy King, Llanstadwell

Susan Kingdom-Wainwright

Mr Aubrey Lawrence & Mrs M. Lawrence

With love to Mary & Clive Lewis

Gaynor & John Lewis, Whitland

David Llewellyn

Mrs P. R. Llewellyn

David Llewhellin

Mr D. & Mrs S. E. Lumb

Brian Maggs, Southcliffe Hotel

R. I. & P. Main, Pembroke Dock

The Malins Family, Saundersfoot

Mr D. G. & Mrs H. Martin, Newport

Mrs P. M. Moody

Graham Leslie Moore

Joan & Alun Morgan, Nyth Aderyn, Tenby

S. M. Mosson & Mr and Mrs L. J. Mosson

Graham Muir & Susan Muir

Sue & Barry Newland, Acton Burnell

Avis Nixon born Tenby 1935

N. D. Osborne, Coseley Bilston, W. Midlands

Charlie & Lorna Parker, Tenby

A. J. & Ivy H. Parker, Coates, Glos.

Donald Price, Tenby

Ian Stuart Prout

Mrs J. A. Pryce

Adrian S. Pyart, Saundersfoot

Mr F. D. & Mrs C. E. Raw, Jameston

Ros, Chris & Em Richards - For Us All

Stanley T. Richards, Tenby

Gwyneth Shaw

Pauline Shipcott

SOO - Tenby

Nancy, Karen, Michelle Stafford & J. Austin.

R. A. & J. M. Stevens

Tenby, Narbeth and Whitland Observer

Caroline & Huw Thomas

Nigel & Jo Tolley

Trevor on your 65th Birthday 5th May 2004

Mr B. & Mrs S. Turnbull, Manorbier

B. M. Turner, Tenby

Valerie Walker

Keith & Joyce Walker of Penally

Dorothy B. White

Martin J. White, Bath

Whitehall Lodge Guest House, Tenby

Hilary Virginia Whittaker

Mr D. G. & Mrs M. Whittle, Sale, Cheshire

D. C. L. Wiffen

Gerald Williams, Penally

Pamela Louie Williams

T. R. Wood, Tenby

FRITH PRODUCTS & SERVICES

Francis Frith would doubtless be pleased to know that the pioneering publishing venture he started in 1860 still continues today. Over a hundred and forty years later, The Francis Frith Collection continues in the same innovative tradition and is now one of the foremost publishers of vintage photographs in the world. Some of the current activities include:

INTERIOR DECORATION

Today Frith's photographs can be seen framed and as giant wall murals in thousands of pubs, restaurants, hotels, banks, retail stores and other public buildings throughout the country. In every case they enhance the unique local atmosphere of the places they depict and provide reminders of gentler days in an increasingly busy and frenetic world.

PRODUCT PROMOTIONS

Frith products are used by many major companies to promote the sales of their own products or to reinforce their own history and heritage. Frith promotions have been used by Hovis bread, Courage beers, Scots Porage Oats, Colman's mustard, Cadbury's foods, Mellow Birds coffee, Dunhill pipe tobacco, Guinness, and Bulmer's Cider.

GENEALOGY AND FAMILY HISTORY

As the interest in family history and roots grows world-wide, more and more people are turning to Frith's photographs of Great Britain for images of the towns, villages and streets where their ancestors lived; and, of course, photographs of the churches and chapels where their ancestors were christened, married and buried are an essential part of every genealogy tree and family album.

FRITH PRODUCTS

All Frith photographs are available Framed or just as Mounted Prints and unmounted versions. These may be ordered from the address below. Other products available are - Calendars, Jigsaws, Canvas Prints, Mugs, Tea Towels, Tableware and local and prestige books.

THE INTERNET

Over several hundred thousand Frith photographs can be viewed and purchased on the internet through the Frith websites!

For more detailed information on Frith products, look at **www.francisfrith.com**

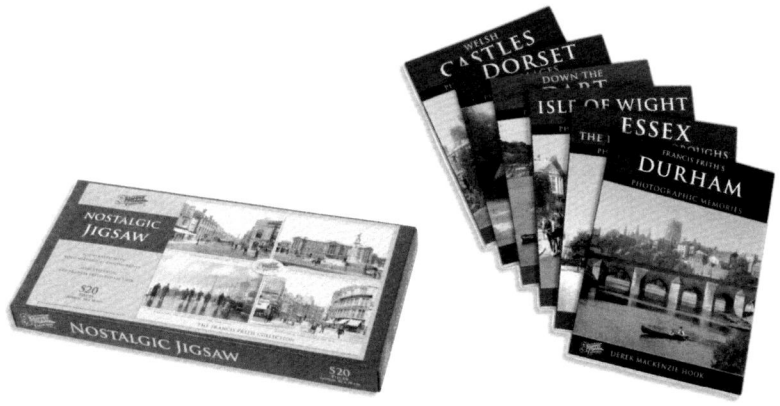

See the complete list of Frith Books at: www.francisfrith.com
This web site is regularly updated with the latest list of publications from The Francis Frith Collection. If you wish to buy books relating to another part of the country that your local bookshop does not stock, you may purchase on-line.

For further information, trade, or author enquiries please contact us at the address below:
The Francis Frith Collection, Unit 19 Kingsmead Business Park, Gillingham, Dorset SP8 5FB.
Tel: +44 (0)1722 716 376   Email: sales@francisfrith.co.uk

See Frith products on the internet at www.francisfrith.com

FREE PRINT OF YOUR CHOICE
CHOOSE A PHOTOGRAPH FROM THIS BOOK
+ POSTAGE

Mounted Print
Overall size 14 x 11 inches (355 x 280mm)

TO RECEIVE YOUR FREE PRINT

Choose any Frith photograph in this book

Simply complete the Voucher opposite and return it with your payment (to cover postage and handling) and we will print the photograph of your choice in SEPIA (size 11 x 8 inches) and supply it in a cream mount ready to frame (overall size 14 x 11 inches).

Order additional Mounted Prints at HALF PRICE - £19.00 each (normally £38.00)

If you would like to order more Frith prints from this book, possibly as gifts for friends and family, you can buy them at half price (with no additional postage costs).

Have your Mounted Prints framed

For an extra £20.00 per print you can have your mounted print(s) framed in an elegant polished wood and gilt moulding, overall size 16 x 13 inches (no additional postage required).

IMPORTANT!

❶ Please note: aerial photographs and photographs with a reference number starting with a "Z" are not Frith photographs and cannot be supplied under this offer.

❷ Offer valid for delivery to one UK address only.

❸ These special prices are only available if you use this form to order. You must use the ORIGINAL VOUCHER on this page (no copies permitted). We can only despatch to one UK address.

❹ This offer cannot be combined with any other offer.

As a customer your name & address will be stored by Frith but not sold or rented to third parties. Your data will be used for the purpose of this promotion only.

Send completed Voucher form to:
**The Francis Frith Collection,
1 Chilmark Estate House, Chilmark,
Salisbury, Wiltshire SP3 5DU**

Voucher for **FREE** and Reduced Price Frith Prints

Please do not photocopy this voucher. Only the original is valid, so please fill it in, cut it out and return it to us with your order.

Picture ref no	Page no	Qty	Mounted @ £19.00	Framed + £20.00	Total Cost £
		1	Free of charge*	£	£
			£19.00	£	£
			£19.00	£	£
			£19.00	£	£
			£19.00	£	£
			£19.00	£	£

*Please allow 28 days for delivery.
Offer available to one UK address only.*

* Post & handling £3.80

Total Order Cost £

Title of this book ....

I enclose a cheque/postal order for £ ....
made payable to 'Heritage Resource Management Ltd'

OR please debit my Mastercard / Visa / Maestro card, details below

Card Number:

Issue No (Maestro only):   Valid from (Maestro):

Card Security Number: Expires:

Signature:

Name Mr/Mrs/Ms ....
Address ....
....
....
.... Postcode ....
Daytime Tel No ....
Email ....

Valid to 31/12/26

Can you help us with information about any of the Frith photographs in this book?

We are gradually compiling an historical record for each of the photographs in the Frith archive. It is always fascinating to find out the names of the people shown in the pictures, as well as insights into the shops, buildings and other features depicted.

If you recognize anyone in the photographs in this book, or if you have information not already included in the author's caption, do let us know. We would love to hear from you, and will try to publish it in future books or articles.

An Invitation from The Francis Frith Collection to Share Your Memories

The 'Share Your Memories' feature of our website allows members of the public to add personal memories relating to the places featured in our photographs, or comment on others already added. Seeing a place from your past can rekindle forgotten or long held memories. Why not visit the website, find photographs of places you know well and add YOUR story for others to read and enjoy? We would love to hear from you!

www.francisfrith.com/memories

Our production team

Frith books are produced by a small dedicated team at offices near Salisbury. Most have worked with the Frith Collection for many years. All have in common one quality: they have a passion for the Frith Collection.

Frith Books and Gifts

We have a wide range of books and gifts available on our website utilising our photographic archive, many of which can be individually personalised.

www.francisfrith.com